My Buddhist Year

Cath Senker

HODDER
Wayland

an imprint of Hodder Children's Books

Titles in this series
My Buddhist Year • My Christian Year • My Hindu Year
My Jewish Year • My Muslim Year • My Sikh Year

Conceived and produced for Hodder Wayland by

Nutshell
MEDIA

Intergen House, 65–67 Western Road, Hove, BN3 2JQ, UK
www.nutshellmedialtd.co.uk

Editor: Alison Cooper
Inside designer and illustrator: Peta Morey
Cover designer: Tim Mayer
Consultants: The Clear Vision Trust, The London Buddhist Vihara, Jim Belither and the Venerable Kelsang Rabten.

Published in Great Britain in 2003 by Hodder Wayland, an imprint of Hodder Children's Books.

British Library Cataloguing in Publication Data
Senker, Cath
My Buddhist year. – (A year of religious festivals)
1. Fasts and feasts – Buddhism – Juvenile literature
294.3'436

ISBN 0 7502 4058 X

Printed in Hong Kong by Wing King Tong.

Hodder Children's Books
A division of Hodder Headline Limited
338 Euston Road, London NW1 3BH

Acknowledgements: The author would like to thank Carolina Rivas McQuire, Kelsang Shraddha, The Clear Vision Trust, the London Buddhist Vihara, Kishani Jayasinghe, the Venerable Kelsang Rabten and Jim Belither for all their help in the preparation of this book.

Note: The diary writer in this book, Carolina, is from the New Kadampa Tradition of Buddhism (NKT), an international Mahayana form of Buddhism that adapts to the culture of the country in which it is practised.

Picture Acknowledgements:
Art Directors & Trip Photo Library 11 (J. Moscrop), 27 (H. Rogers); Britstock 16 (Shiro Daifu), 17 (Sakae Arai); Chapel Studios 22 (Zul Mukhida); Circa Photo Library 6 (Tjalling Halbertsma), 8, 15, 19 (William Holtby); Clear Vision 12, 13, 18 (Mokshajyoti); Eye Ubiquitous *Cover* (David Cumming), 4 (Paul Seheult), 7 (Tim Page), 14 (Paul Seheult), 20 (Tim Page), 25 (Julia Waterlow), 26 (Tim Page); London Buddhist Vihara 21; Nutshell Media 5 (Yiorgos Nikiteas); Robert Harding Picture Library *Title page*, 9, 24; Tibet Images 10 (Ian Cumming), 23 (Robin Bath).

Cover photograph: A young Buddhist monk in Myanmar (Burma).
Title page: Young monks in Myanmar carrying the food offerings they have been given.

Contents

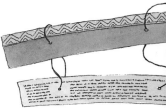

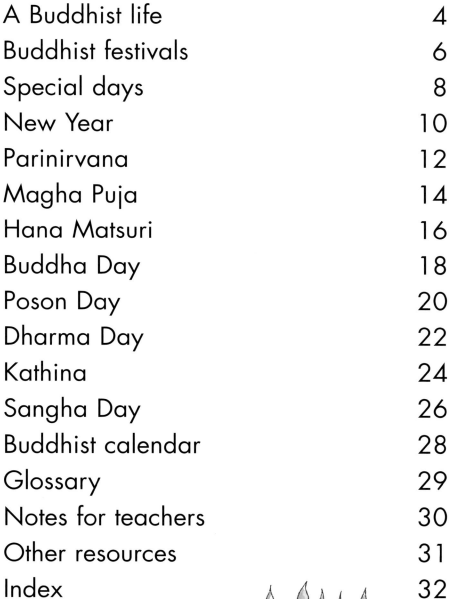

A Buddhist life

Buddhists follow the Buddha's teachings.
The Buddha was a great holy man.
He lived 2,500 years ago.

Buddhists follow some simple rules in their lives. They try not to kill or hurt living things. They try not to take anything they haven't been given. They aim to tell the truth and keep a clear mind. They try not to be greedy.

This is a statue of the Buddha at a temple in Thailand. The Buddha is always shown as calm and peaceful.

This is Carolina outside her Buddhist centre. She has written a diary about the Buddhist festivals.

Carolina's diary
Saturday 14 July

My name's Carolina and I'm 8 and a bit. My mum and I used to live in the Buddhist centre but now we live in a big shared house. We've got loads of pets – a dog, two chickens, two goldfish and three cats. I really love horse-riding, even though I've only been a couple of times.

The Pali Canon is the oldest collection of Buddhist holy books. It contains the Buddha's teachings.

The Buddhist symbol is called the Wheel of Dharma.

Buddhist festivals

Buddhist festivals are joyful times. People enjoy meeting together at a Buddhist centre or temple. Everyone thinks about their beliefs and how to become a kinder person.

There are many different Buddhist festivals around the world. The most important ones celebrate events in the Buddha's life.

These Buddhist monks in Mongolia are celebrating the opening of a new monastery.

These girls in Sri Lanka are dressed in white for Poson Day.

Some festivals are special to a particular country. For example, Sri Lankans celebrate Poson Day. All Buddhists celebrate Wesak, or Buddha Day.

Carolina's diary
Sunday 15 August

We've just got back from our summer festival. It's my favourite Buddhist festival. It's for two weeks every year and we go camping. At the campsite there are two big trees that I love climbing! I always meet lots of other children there who are Buddhists as well.

Special days

Every month

Every month, most Buddhists have special religious days. These are often days when there is a full moon. Many Buddhists go to the temple to worship.

Buddhist worship is called puja. People chant to show their love for the Buddha. They make offerings of flowers, candles, incense and pure water at a shrine. People thank the Buddha for his teachings.

This man is worshipping in the shrine room of his Buddhist centre.

In Colombo, Sri Lanka, there is a special ceremony on every full moon day.

Carolina's diary
Sunday 29 December

Yesterday was Lama Chopa (you say 'Larma Cherpa'). This is a special day that happens every two weeks. I went to the children's group at the Buddhist centre. We heard a story about the Buddha and talked about what it meant. We sang prayers. Afterwards, we offered vegetarian food to the Buddha. We imagined him eating it. Then we had a feast and ate it ourselves!

A Buddhist teacher gives a talk and people meditate. They sit quietly and try to become still, relaxed and peaceful.

New Year

January, February, March or April

New Year is a good time for making a new start. Buddhists think about how to be more kind and generous to others. They may go to the temple to worship.

In Tibet, Buddhists spring clean their homes for a fresh new start to the year. Then there are three days of feasting, dancing and sports. After this there are more serious ceremonies.

In Tibet, prayers written on coloured flags are hung up as part of the New Year celebrations.

In this village in China, women are taking part in a New Year dance.

Carolina's diary
Friday 3 January

We held a puja on Wednesday to celebrate the New Year. I think of New Year like this: we believe in the power of karma, or actions. If you do kind things, you'll enjoy the results. You'll make the world a better place. For me, New Year is a time for looking at the last year and seeing how I could do better this year. Then I can make a fresh start.

In China, Sri Lanka and Thailand, people also hold religious ceremonies. They enjoy special food, traditional games, processions, music and dancing.

Parinirvana

February

At this festival people remember the death of the Buddha. When he was 81 years old, the Buddha knew that the time had come for him to die. He lay down and died peacefully.

A painting of the death of the Buddha. The Buddha died with his friends gathered around him.

On this shrine, for Parinirvana, there are photos of loved ones who have died.

In the temple, the lights may be lowered. People chant and meditate in the dimmed light. Then the lights are made bright again. The lights are a symbol. They show that the light of the Buddha's teachings continues to shine in the world.

Carolina's diary
Sunday 15 February

My friend Ella invited me to visit her Western Buddhist centre for Parinirvana. We heard a story about the last days of the Buddha's life. Then we talked about people we knew who had died. We put photos of them on the shrine. We always say special prayers for people who are dying so their next life will be good.

Magha Puja

February

At Magha Puja, Buddhists in Thailand and other countries remember an important event in the Buddha's life. This was when 1,250 of his followers came to see him.

He said they should try to be kind, generous and patient. He said they should not harm living things.

In Thailand, people light candles and incense sticks at Magha Puja.

This young monk is meditating. Meditation is an important part of Buddhist life, and all festivals.

To celebrate Magha Puja, Buddhists go to their temple. In large temples, 1,250 candles are lit to remember the Buddha's followers.

Carolina's diary
Friday 28 February

Buddhists don't all celebrate the same festivals. Mum and I are NKT Buddhists. We don't celebrate Magha Puja, but we do celebrate the teachings the Buddha gave to his followers. Every month there is the Kangso prayer. It celebrates our rules for everyday life. I don't go because it's four hours long and I'd get tired, but Mum does.

Hana Matsuri

8 April

Hana Matsuri is a Japanese festival. It celebrates the Buddha's birth. Buddhists wash a statue of the baby Buddha in perfumed water or sweet tea. They hang a garland of flowers around his neck.

The statue is paraded through the streets. Everyone throws lotus flowers into the path of the procession. Then there is a lively fair.

Children wear traditional Japanese clothes for the Hana Matsuri festival in Japan.

Carolina's diary

Tuesday 8 April

My friend Momo is Japanese. Today was Hana Matsuri and she e-mailed me about it. It's her favourite festival. She visited the temple, and there was a hall filled with colourful flowers. It looked like the beautiful garden where the Buddha was born. Inside was a lovely statue of the baby Buddha. Momo helped to pour sweet tea on the Buddha's head.

These children are joining in with the folk dancing at Hana Matsuri.

People set up stalls to sell food. There is folk dancing, and acrobats perform to the crowd.

Buddha Day

May

Buddha Day, or Wesak, is a very important Buddhist festival. It celebrates the Buddha's Enlightenment.

When the Buddha became Enlightened, his mind became clear and peaceful. He knew how to be kind to others, and how to help people to be happy.

This boy in Britain is lighting a candle at Wesak. The shrine is often specially decorated for the festival.

These Buddhists in Nepal are lighting lamps to celebrate Wesak.

At Wesak, Buddhists visit their temple for worship. Money or food may be given to poor people, and to Buddhist monks and nuns. Some Western Buddhists bring food and share a meal together.

Carolina's diary
Tuesday 15 April

Today was our Buddha Day. We went to the Buddhist centre to be blessed. We were given a little woollen bracelet. Sometimes we get a crystal. We looked at it to remember the Buddha's Enlightenment, and to remember to love others. I'm going to wear my bracelet until it wears out. Then I'll put it on my shrine.

Poson Day

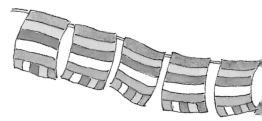

June

Poson celebrates the time when Buddhism came to Sri Lanka. Buddhists from Sri Lanka go to their temple. They listen to a talk. Then they chant and meditate together.

People make offerings and give money to the temple. It is a time to be especially generous.

These pilgrims have come to Mihintale, in Sri Lanka, to worship on Poson Day.

The Buddhist flag is raised outside a Buddhist temple in Britain for Poson Day.

Carolina's diary
Monday 24 June

Yesterday was Poson Day. My mum's friend Sarah told me how it was celebrated at a London temple. Lots of Sri Lankan people go there. At 9 a.m., they raised the Buddhist flag outside the temple. It was a very happy moment. After puja, chanting and meditation they listened to a talk. Afterwards they drank lots of tea and shared tasty Sri Lankan food.

In Sri Lanka, some people go on a pilgrimage to a place called Mihintale. This is where Buddhism first arrived in the country, over 2,000 years ago. An Indian prince told the king of Sri Lanka all about it.

Dharma Day

July

Dharma Day celebrates the first time the Buddha gave his teachings, called Dharma. Dharma means 'truth'.

Buddhists believe that having things doesn't make people truly happy. They practise meditation. It helps them to understand that real happiness comes from learning to be happy with whatever we have, or whatever we are doing.

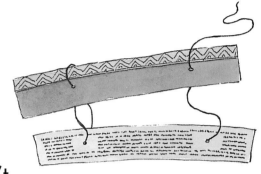

This monk is reading a story from the Pali Canon, which was written on strips of palm leaf.

These Tibetan boys are training to be monks. Reading the Buddha's teachings is an important part of their training.

On Dharma Day Buddhists go to their temple. Children may listen to stories from the Pali Canon. They hear the Buddha's teachings about giving and sharing things.

Carolina's diary
Wednesday 6 July

Friday was our Dharma Day. We celebrated the Buddha's teachings spreading all over the world. We held a special puja. The Buddha taught people how to work things out for themselves rather than telling them what to do. Last week my friends were planning to run away from school. I talked to them about their reasons. In the end they didn't leave.

Kathina

October or November

Kathina celebrates Buddhist monks and nuns. It began in Asia. Kathina comes at the end of the rainy season in Asia.

In Eastern countries, Buddhists look after the monks and nuns. They give them everything they need. This includes food, new robes and shelter. Buddhists like to be generous.

These young monks in Burma are carrying the food offerings they have been given.

During the rainy season, monks and nuns stay in monasteries. When the rains stop, people give them new robes.

These monks are looking at the cloth they have been given to make new robes for Kathina.

Carolina's diary

Wednesday 27 October

It's good having a mum who's a Buddhist nun. When we're out, everyone can see that she's a nun, so she can't shout at me! Also, she's much calmer than she was before she became a nun. People don't give her new robes but they help in other ways. Last year, they gave her money so she could go to New York for some special teachings.

Sangha Day

November

Sangha Day is a celebration of friendship. The Sangha is the Buddhist community. People like to gather with their Buddhist friends and teachers. They celebrate the love and support they give each other.

These children in Britain are meditating at their Buddhist centre on Sangha Day.

Everyone enjoys having a meal together on Sangha Day.

On Sangha Day, people go to their temple. They may read from the Buddhist holy books and meditate.

Many people do puja and listen to a talk by a Buddhist teacher. Everyone enjoys a shared meal.

Carolina's diary
Sunday 9 November

Today was Sangha Day. We call it NKT Temples Day. We have temples in different countries where everyone can pray for world peace. On Sangha Day we do things to raise money for the temples. This year we had a show with people doing silly acts. You could pay money to throw cream pies at them! It was really funny. Then we shared loads of food.

Buddhist calendar

January/February/March/April
(1 day to 3 weeks in different countries)

Buddhist New Year

Buddhists think about how to be kinder and more generous to people.

February (full moon day)

Magha Puja

People remember how 1,250 followers came to the Buddha and were given a special talk.

February (full moon day)

Parinirvana

A festival held in memory of the death of the Buddha.

8 April

Hana Matsuri

A Japanese celebration of the Buddha's birthday.

May (full moon day)

Buddha Day or Wesak

An important festival to celebrate the Buddha's Enlightenment.

June (full moon day)

Poson Day

On this day people remember Buddhism coming to Sri Lanka.

July (full moon day)

Dharma Day

A celebration of the first time the Buddha gave his teachings.

July/August (2 weeks)

NKT summer festival

NKT Buddhists gather to listen to teachings and learn about the Buddhist way of life.

October/November (1 day)

Kathina

A ceremony for giving new robes to monks and nuns.

November (full moon day)

Sangha Day

Buddhists come together to celebrate their worldwide community, the Sangha.

Glossary

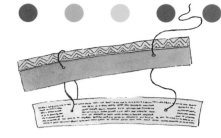

Buddha The Buddha was called Siddhartha Gautama when he was born. After he attained Enlightenment he became known as the Buddha. The Buddha means 'the one who understands the truth'.

chant A prayer with a few words that are sung over and over again.

Dharma The truth. It also means the Buddha's teaching.

Enlightenment Being perfectly kind and generous, understanding the world completely and being fearless.

incense A stick that is burned to give off a nice smell.

karma This means action.

meditate To sit quietly and still with your thoughts so you can become calm, happy and wise.

monastery A special place where monks live together.

NKT The New Kadampa Tradition of Buddhism. It has many centres in Europe, the Americas and Asia.

offerings Food, flowers or other gifts that are placed in front of statues of the Buddha to give thanks for his teachings.

Pali Canon The oldest collection of Buddhist writings, from Sri Lanka.

pilgrims People who make a special journey to a holy place.

puja Worship.

robes Long, simple clothes, like the Buddha's clothes, that are worn by monks and nuns.

Sangha The group of people who follow the Buddha's teachings. Sometimes it is used to mean only monks and nuns.

shrine A place where people come to worship. It usually has an image of the Buddha. Many Buddhists have small shrines at home where they worship alone.

temple A building where Buddhists meet for worship. Some Buddhists call their temple a vihara. Others meet at a Buddhist centre.

vegetarian food Food made without meat or fish.

Western Buddhist A Buddhist who is not from an Asian family. Western Buddhists may practise Buddhism in a different way from Asian Buddhists.

Notes for teachers

pp4–5 Together these guidelines form the Five Precepts, which are all expressions of the principle of non-harm – the basis of Buddhist ethics. Buddhists try to cultivate an attitude of heartfelt loving-kindness to all living things. They often hold jobs that do not exploit people or the planet, and many train their minds through regular meditation. These are some of the areas of life covered by the Eightfold Path, which is symbolized by the Wheel of the Dharma. Buddhists do not worship the Buddha as a god; they use his image to remind them of his qualities, which they try to emulate. The Buddha taught that all people could achieve the perfection of Enlightenment if they made the effort to change.

pp6–7 There are many styles and forms of Buddhism, each with different festivals. Some festivals are specific to certain countries as well as to particular traditions in Buddhism. This is because when Buddhism spread from India around the world, it integrated with the cultures and religions already existing in each country. Yet the teachings of the Buddha remain the same, regardless of the cultural form that Buddhism takes.

pp8–9 Lama Chopa (NKT tradition) is ten days after every full moon and new moon. On religious days, especially full moon days, adult Buddhists may follow extra rules. For example, because Buddhists believe in reincarnation, they might fast from midday on a religious day, to purify themselves of unkind actions in previous lives. The offerings have various meanings, for example: flowers, which wilt, remind people that everything changes; candles represent the Buddha's teaching, which lights up the world; the scent of incense spreads around the room, a symbol that good actions have an effect on the world. Food offerings are regarded as special food that helps people to become pure. Many Buddhists also have a shrine at home.

pp10–11 Buddhist New Year traditions vary greatly. In Britain, the Friends of the Western Buddhist Order (FWBO) celebrate on 1 January; they may go on retreat at the Buddhist centre, meditate and enjoy spending time together. New Year is the biggest festival for Buddhists in Tibet; it can last for up to fifteen days. In countries such as Thailand, Burma and Sri Lanka, New Year is celebrated for two or three days over the first full moon

day in April. In Sri Lanka there is a detailed timetable of what people should do at specific times over the festival, including when food should be cooked, when children play traditional games, and when people pay respects to their elders and exchange gifts.

pp12–13 The Buddha spent the last 35 years of his life travelling around India and giving his teaching to all who would listen; many people joined the Buddhist Sangha (community). When he knew that he was about to die, the Buddha called his followers to him and asked them if they understood all his teachings properly. Carolina's friend belongs to the Friends of the Western Buddhist Order, who mark the death of the Buddha with the ceremonies of Parinirvana. When someone dies, Buddhists pray the person will have a fortunate next life.

pp14–15 Buddhists believe that everyone has the potential to become a Buddha, and the way to reach Buddhahood is through practice. The Buddha taught that people should practise compassion and kindness towards other beings, along with developing wisdom – an understanding of the true nature of life.

pp16–17 Lotus flowers are significant in Buddhism. The lotus rises out of the muddy water into the sunlight. Similarly people's minds, through practising kindness and developing wisdom, can change from being muddied by greedy and selfish thoughts to being beautifully clear. At Hana Matsuri, displays in the grounds of Buddhist temples remind people of the Buddha's birth story: the gods told Queen Maya that she was going to give birth to the Buddha. On the way to her parents' house to have the baby, she visited a beautiful garden and her baby was born there.

pp18–19 The title 'Buddha' means 'one who is fully awake'. The Buddha became Enlightened; he became free from suffering and gained an understanding of the way things really are. Practising generosity is important. It can involve helping people or helping in the Buddhist centre, not only giving money or food. The festival varies in different traditions. Some Buddhists remember the Buddha's birth and death at Wesak. At all festivals, people renew their commitment to the Buddhist way of life.

pp20–21 About 250 years after the Buddha's death, the Indian emperor Asoka converted to Buddhism, and the religion began to spread around India. The emperor sent monks to Sri Lanka, Nepal and Tibet, too. In 246 BCE, Arahant Mahinda, the son of the emperor, brought Buddhism to Sri Lanka. Carolina is describing how Poson Day is celebrated at the London Buddhist Vihara, or temple, where the Sri Lankan Buddhist traditions are followed. Poson Day is not celebrated by the NKT tradition.

pp22–23 When the Buddha became Enlightened, he revealed the Four Noble Truths, fundamental to Buddhist teaching: 1. All life involves suffering, or dissatisfaction; 2. The ordinary things we desire do not last and cannot make us happy, so we experience suffering; 3. Suffering can be ended; 4. It can be ended by following the Eightfold Path (see pp4–5), which leads to Enlightenment. For 400 years after the Buddha's death the sermons, stories and rules of conduct contained in the Pali Canon were passed on orally. Then they were written down in the Pali language, on strips of palm leaf. Today the Pali Canon is published in book format, in many different languages.

pp24–25 Monks and nuns dedicate themselves to the Buddhist way of life. They wear special robes and live in monasteries. In the West, many very committed Buddhists do not become monks and nuns. They may wear ordinary clothes and live in Buddhist communities, or at home with their families, or alone. They usually work for a living. Carolina's mum, Shraddha, became a nun when Carolina was 6. Now that she is a nun she will remain single.

pp26–27 The Sangha is one of the three jewels of Buddhism to which all Buddhists commit: the Buddha (their teacher), the Dharma (his teaching) and the Sangha (the Buddhist community). The Sangha includes all those who follow the Buddha's teaching – monks, nuns and lay people, although in southern Asia the term is often used to refer only to monks and nuns. On Sangha Day, members of the Friends of the Western Buddhist Order renew their commitment. NKT Buddhists undertake fundraising events like the one Carolina describes.

p28 Buddhists follow a lunar calendar and most festivals take place on full moon days. In the West this is sometimes adjusted to a weekend date so more people are able to participate.

Other resources

Artefacts

Articles of Faith, Resource House, Kay Street, Bury, Lancashire BL9 6BU Tel. 0161 763 6232
The Clear Vision Trust, 16–20 Turner Street, Manchester M4 1DZ Tel. 0161 839 9579
Religion in Evidence, 28b Nunn Brook Road Industrial Estate, Huthwaite, Nottinghamshire NG17 2HU Tel. 0800 318686

Books to read

Celebrations! Wesak by Anita Ganeri (Heinemann, 2001)
I am a Buddhist by D. Samaraesekara (Franklin Watts, 2001)
My Buddhist Faith by Adiccabandhu (Evans, 1999)
Places of Worship: Buddhist Temples by Andrea Wilson (Heinemann, 2000)
The Monkey King, Siddhartha and the Swan, The Lion and the Jackal, all by Padmasri and Adiccabandhu (Windhorse Publications/The Clear Vision Trust ,1998)
What Do We Know About Buddhism? by Sue Elford (Hodder Wayland, 2001)

Photopack

Living Religions: Buddhism posterpack and booklet by Thomas Nelson and Sons.

Videos

Animated World Faiths Video for ages 7–12. (Channel 4)
Buddhism Video and teachers' handbook for KS2. (The Clear Vision Trust)
The Monkey King Video and book package. (The Clear Vision Trust)
Stop, Look and Listen: 'Water, Moon, Candle, Tree and Sword' Video for KS 1 (Channel 4)

Websites

For websites that are relevant to this book, go to: www.waylinks.co.uk/yearfestivalsbuddhist

Index